In memory of

Hattie Thornton Hayes,

Ashland's first librarian.

JACKSON COUNTY
Library Services

Rookie
Read-About Science®

Our Living Forests

By Allan Fowler

Consultants

Linda Cornwell, Learning Resource Consultant,
Indiana Department of Education

Sharyn Fenwick, Elementary Science/Math Specialist,
Gustavus Adolphus College, St. Peter, Minnesota

Janann V. Jenner, Ph.D.

Children's Press®

Visit Children's Press® on the Internet at:
http://publishing.grolier.com

Designer: Herman Adler Design Group

Library of Congress Cataloging-in-Publication Data

Fowler, Allan.
    Our living forests / by Allan Fowler.
      p. cm. – (Rookie read-about science)
    Includes index.
    Summary: Describes different types of forests and some of the kinds of trees that
grow in them, as well as the animals that live there and threats to their existence.
    ISBN 0-516-20811-X (lib. bdg.)   0-516-26481-8 (pbk.)
    1. Forests and forestry—Juvenile literature. 2. Forest ecology—Juvenile
literature. [1. Forests and forestry.] I. Title. II. Series.
SD376.F685   1999   97-31669
578.73—dc21   CIP
                                                  AC

Imagine standing in a California redwood forest. The trees are so tall and so close together that you can hardly see the sky.

4

Imagine flying over the Great Smoky Mountains of Tennessee and North Carolina.

You would be looking down on a carpet of thick green forest covering the rounded hills.

There are many
beautiful forest areas
all over the world.

The kinds of trees you find
in each forest depend on
the weather and soil there.

Evergreen forests grow in
places that are usually cool.

Evergreens have needles instead of leaves and are never bare. As they shed their needles, new ones grow. This is why they are called evergreens.

Other kinds of trees
drop their leaves every
fall, stay bare all winter,

Fall

Winter

10

Spring

Summer

grow new leaves in spring,
and stay green all summer.

11

Before the leaves drop off
in September or October,
their colors change to
shades of red, yellow,
orange, or brown.

People make special trips just to see these colors, especially where maple forests blaze bright red.

Most trees that shed their leaves have hard wood. People make furniture from hardwood trees, such as oak, hickory, or walnut.

Hickory

Cypresses

In warm places, you find forests of southern pines, cypresses, live oaks, and flowering magnolias.

15

The giant evergreens of the far west grow tall because of heavy rains. Some may be 4,000 years old.

The coast redwoods of California are the tallest trees in the world. Some reach as high as thirty-story buildings.

The thickest kind of forest is a rain forest. Most rain forests grow in very warm places, such as the Amazon Valley of South America.

Olympic National Park, in Washington State, has an evergreen rain forest. It rains there more than in any other part of the United States.

Below the treetops, forests are full of life. Plants, such as vines, shrubs, ferns, and flowers, grow in forests.

Moss may cover the ground
in redwood forests.

White-tailed deer

Forests are filled with animal life, such as insects, birds, deer, foxes, squirrels, mice, and other animals.

Red fox

The trees provide
food for the animals.

They eat leaves, fruit,
nuts, acorns, and seeds.

There used to be many more forests.

But people and nature can threaten a forest's survival. People cut down many trees.

Insects and diseases also destroy trees. Careless people and lightning can start forest fires.

Today, people take great care to keep our woodlands alive. When trees are cut down, new ones are planted. Forest rangers watch for fires.

The United States and Canadian Forest Services have set aside large forest areas—to be enjoyed, not disturbed.

Words You Know

moss

needles

rain forest

cypresses

evergreens

redwoods

31

Index

About the Author

Allan Fowler is a freelance writer with a background in advertising. Born in New York, he now lives in Chicago and enjoys traveling.

Photo Credits

©: Bob Clemenz Photography: 16 (Bob & Suzanne Clemenz); Dembinsky Photo Assoc.: 26 (John Mielcarek); Donald J. Leopold: 3, 4, 6, 8, 9, 12, 13, 14, 15, 22, 29, 30 top right, 31; Photo Researchers: 10, 11 (Jan Halaska), 18, 30 bottom (Jacques Jangoux), cover, 23 (Stephen J. Krasemann), 25 (Jeff Lepore), 7 (Tom & Pat Lesson), 24 (Gregory K. Scott), 19, 20 (Jim Steinberg), 21, 30 top left (David Weintraub).